Meditation

The Fundamental Principles Of Meditation For Novices Seeking Stress Relief Through This Discipline As A Therapeutic Technique To Enhance Spirituality And Vitality

Vincent Chisholm

TABLE OF CONTENT

Introduction To Meditation 1

The Interconnectedness of Affection and Empathy 7

Choosing A Mantra 29

What Hypnosis Is And What It Is Not And What Benefits It Has On Insomnia Disorder 49

Embrace The Present Moment While Engaging In The Practice Of Meditation. 78

Exercise 88

Mindfulness Meditation 111

The Enhancing Effects Of Meditation On Quality Of Life 121

Guided Meditations For Love 127

Introduction To Meditation

Given the complexities and relentless nature of contemporary lifestyles, it is inescapable that numerous individuals experience feelings of stress and excessive workloads. It often gives the sense that a single day is inadequate to accomplish all tasks. Our stress and fatigue readily engender feelings of frustration, sadness, and impatience. Our well-being may also be jeopardized. We are overwhelmed with our commitments such that we perceive a lack of opportunity to pause and engage in meditation. A lesser-known fact is that meditation offers the advantage of time expansion, achieved through the cultivation of a tranquil and focused state of mind.

Meditation is increasingly being recognized as a highly effective methodology for individuals to alleviate and untangle their minds from the various stressors that accompany daily existence. Numerous individuals engage in meditation with varied motivations, ranging from assuaging and remedying physical, mental, and emotional strain to attaining elevated states of consciousness and self-actualization.

An illustrated portrayal from The New Yorker encapsulates the essence of meditation through a straightforward depiction: Two monks are engaged in a seated position, engaged in the practice of meditation. The younger individual is giving the older individual a perplexed glance, prompting the older individual to assert, "Subsequent events are devoid of any significance." This marks the culmination of individuals' varying perspectives towards meditation. Certain individuals may envision monks who are engaged in peaceful contemplation while gathered in isolated locations. There exists a belief among certain individuals that engaging in meditation is tantamount to engaging in prayer or engaging in acts of worship, however, this claim is unfounded. An alternative stance exists wherein individuals perpetuate a misrepresentation or obfuscation by associating it with the realms of music or art.

The true essence of meditation lies in cultivating a state of mindfulness and tranquility in one's every endeavor. Several of the most efficacious methods for practicing it include engaging in breath counting, attentively observing the sounds of the natural environment, and participating in various pursuits that do not agitate the mind. Meditation involves the disciplined cultivation of directing one's attention towards a singular point of reference. It entails directing your attention towards your breath, physical sensations, or a specific word or phrase referred to as a mantra. In essence, meditation involves shifting one's attention away from any divergent thoughts and directing it towards the immediate present moment. One can achieve this by assuming a seated posture, closing the eyes, and directing their attention towards the task of calming the mind.

This method of reflection and contemplation can be adopted by individuals encountering problems, anxiety, and stress, regardless of their background or capabilities. Engaging in a brief mindfulness practice of ten to fifteen minutes focused on deep breathing could potentially facilitate the alleviation of stress, the attainment of equilibrium, and the cultivation of a sense of serenity within oneself.

Mind-training can be achieved through both sedentary and active practices, which may involve the utilization of ceremonial items such as prayer beads to effectively monitor one's daily endeavors. Demonstrating steadfast dedication is essential in managing the overall well-being, including the challenges associated with health conditions such as depression or hypertension.

It is equally essential to be aware that improper meditation techniques can potentially inflict harm upon oneself. Meditation has also been acknowledged to exert adverse health implications in certain individuals. They have the potential to encounter symptoms such as muscular contractions, sleeplessness, sensory illusions, or periods of dissociation. Individuals have a propensity for evaluating their unfavorable cognitions and retaining pessimistic sentiments. They demonstrate limited capacity for suppressing distressing memories, encounter challenges in establishing emotional connections, and posess the belief that meditation will aid in resolving their issues. Indeed, the practice of meditation demands unwavering perseverance and steadfast devotion in order to attain one's objectives. However, if you are of the belief that meditation exacerbates the situation, it is recommended that you discontinue the practice immediately.

Meditation not only aids in the alleviation of our mental state, but it also facilitates a deeper comprehension of our own cognition. We can acquire the knowledge and strategies to transition our mindset from negative to positive, from unhappiness to happiness, from turmoil to tranquility. The chief objective of meditation is to overcome negative thoughts and unravel one's true self. It is an immensely advantageous habit that can be savored and indulged in throughout the entirety of the day.

The Interconnectedness of Affection and Empathy

Have you previously experienced being embraced within a compassionate community?

When multiple individuals converge with utmost sincerity, an atmosphere of unconditional affection is established. The aforementioned hearts display a profound receptiveness to their own essence, to one another, and to the divine. The establishment of a love network ensues from the profound alignment of each individual with their innate essence, as well as their unification with the benevolent nourishment and guidance bestowed by the divine. Simultaneously, the cultivation of love is fostered through reciprocal acts of affection and connection among individuals. One of the most profound and exhilarating experiences an individual can encounter in their lifetime is to be embraced within a nurturing community.

Nevertheless, the notion of a love circle is an encounter that is scarce or nonexistent for the overwhelming majority of individuals engaged in romantic partnerships. This phenomenon arises from the circumstance that when the primary objective is to safeguard oneself from pain instead of seeking understanding of love, the heart not only becomes impervious to emotions but also to interpersonal connections and transcendental experiences.

It is highly commendable to exert oneself in the pursuit of cultivating a sphere of affection, as it is an inherently profound endeavor. It is the desire that resonates within the depths of our hearts and souls. Several of the results arising from the circle of love encompass enjoyment, elation, heightened closeness, and enhanced innovation. The issue at hand pertains to the measures that can be undertaken in order to augment the quantity of affectionate relationships in one's life.

The essence of love derives from the innermost essence, the Spirit, and once realized, it has the ability to be imparted to others. If one lacks a connection to the divine, they fail to perceive that it is the divine that bestows its love and sustenance upon them, as they are unable to receive such blessings from the divine. If you are not cognizant of the fact that you are in receipt of this correspondence, you will be unable to perceive the entirety of its contents within the depths of your being. Alternatively, you experience a profound emptiness and profound solitude, leading you to seek solace and fulfillment through the affection of others, yearning for it to assuage the void within you. It is possible that you have been educated to reciprocate affection in order to receive it, yet what you are truly endeavoring to accomplish is to assert authority and dominance over the other person, with the expectation that they will fulfill your perceived needs for emotional security, self-worth, and affection. If one enters into relationships with the objective of seeking love from others, instead of cultivating an inner reservoir of love from a divine source and reciprocating it with others, the profound delight of being enveloped by a communal bond of affection will forever evade their grasp.

What other pursuit in life could conceivably hold greater significance than the ability to partake in an affectionate and interconnected social network with those for whom you hold deep regard? This unparalleled experience is unrivaled by any other. Placing Inner Bonding at the forefront of our obligations is of utmost importance, even though we must unquestionably allocate time and effort towards securing our financial well-being, upholding our physical health, nurturing our unique abilities, and fulfilling the mundane duties that compose our everyday existence. The establishment of a profound and ethereal bond, which forms the foundation for the circle of affection, can be achieved by engaging in the process of inner bonding, a method empirically validated for its efficacy. The primary objective of Inner Bonding is not simply to acquire the ability to love oneself and establish a connection with Spirit, but rather to lay the necessary groundwork in order to engage in the act of love-sharing.

Self-compassion

Love propels us. The concept of ego is inherent within each individual. Our sense of self repeatedly insists: "Myself, myself, myself." "Belonging to me, belonging to me, belonging to me."

Love differs from other emotional experiences. Love transcends mere emotions or sentiments. We are propelled beyond the constraints of the self by a transcendent power.

From this direct perspective, a notable proportion of the spiritual realm does not revolve around otherworldly encounters, the use of aromatic substances for purifying purposes, or participating in expensive withdrawal programs. It entails the development of love as it transcends the boundaries imposed by our individual ego, and expands to encompass increasingly broader circles that embody compassion, gentleness, and vastness. It is highly valuable to dedicate some time to introspection, contemplating upon our own emotions and assessing the depth of our ability to empathize. Towards whom do we direct our efforts throughout our lifetime, seeking their gratification in the final analysis?

Love serves as the impetus that drives us to transition from one smaller, more insular, and self-centered group to the succeeding one. This holds true in all cases.

If our compassion encompasses only ourselves, then our sphere of compassionate understanding has not been sufficiently broadened. It exemplifies a self-centered attitude.

By means of affection, we can transcend the limitations imposed by our egos and prioritize the welfare of others, either before or on par with our own. Our love abounds and stretches beyond our individual selves, encompassing our families, communities, and close companions. Nevertheless, this cannot serve as the ultimate destination. Expand the dimensions of the affectionate sphere.

If our sphere of concern is limited to solely one family, particularly our own, it can be regarded as a manifestation of nepotism.

Love places a higher emphasis on the welfare of a substantial number of households as compared to that of one's own family, however, it must not conclude at that point. Expand the scope of the affectionate sphere.

The manifestation in question can be classified as a type of tribalism when it pertains to a singular group of individuals that falls within the boundaries of our consideration.

Love possesses the capacity to forge a harmonious bond among the disparate populace dwelling within an imaginary demarcation, yet it must not perpetually abide in that state of inertia. Expand the dimensions of the affectionate circle.

Should our nation's capacity for compassion be confined to the limits of its boundaries, we must acknowledge and address the inherent issue at hand: such an extreme manifestation of nationalism.

In the event that the projection extends beyond a national border and instead aligns with the collective devotion of an entire religious community, it also signifies a progression towards the global and the universal. Nonetheless, this cannot serve as the ultimate destination. Expand the dimensions of the affectionate sphere.

Should our capacity for compassion be constrained by the boundaries of a religious community, we are confronted with a critical issue, specifically, an intense manifestation of religious fervor.

It is imperative that we continuously broaden and deepen the sphere of affection, commonly referred to as the circle of love. When every individual within the human race, without any exclusions, is enveloped by the encompassing power of affection. At the point when all individuals, irrespective of their gender, ethnicity, religious beliefs, socioeconomic status, or nationality are genuinely accepted, we will have transcended the limitations imposed by selfishness, favoritism, intense patriotism, and religious extremism, to reach a state that is deserving of our true potential and deserving of affection. This location will be deserving of both of these attributes.

Aids in mitigating the effects of both emotional and physical distress.

The presence of persistent physical pain is capable of exerting a detrimental impact on one's psychological well-being. When one experiences discomfort, there is a possibility of developing stress, thereby exacerbating the experience of suffering. Fortunately, through the practice of meditation, one may experience a significant reduction in the intensity of physical discomfort, potentially up to a 50% decrease.

In addition to causing physical discomfort, the chronic pain also has the potential to adversely impact your mental well-being on occasion. Meditation is instrumental in facilitating the management and cultivation of the ability to effectively address and react to this distress. The present moment can engage your mind, aiding you in approaching challenges with a positive outlook.

Meditation facilitates interpersonal interactions, fostering harmonious cohabitation. One develops the realization that one's happiness cannot be attributed to anyone else. Consequently, you will foster enhanced relationships and empower yourself to sustain them. Additionally, you will acquire the ability to be more appreciative, which in turn will enable you to cultivate self-acceptance.

Assists in attaining authentic happiness

Through meditation, you can achieve real happiness from within you. You shall carry out these actions while taking precautions to ensure the safety and well-being of yourself and others. The happiness of others will never be compromised in order to ensure your own happiness. You can expect a reduction in pain, alleviated concerns, heightened positive emotions, and enhanced satisfaction, coupled with improved overall health.

These advantages are not solely limited to the ones mentioned; there are additional benefits to be gained through the practice of meditation. The meditator is unable to articulate additional advantages. Please be informed that meditation is a cost-free practice, as it does not necessitate the use of any equipment, and can be acquired easily and executed with simplicity. With a mere commitment of 15-20 minutes per session, one can experience transformative shifts in one's existence, pushing boundaries, fostering personal growth, and cultivating a truly gratifying life experience.

Obstacles To Meditation

Have you ever experienced the sensation where, on occasions when you are genuinely intent upon a matter and have exerted your utmost effort towards a plan, concept, or undertaking, a series of adverse circumstances invariably arise? Precisely at the moment you make the determination to alter your dietary habits and abstain from consuming beer, your acquaintances arrive to proffer you beer? And whenever you choose to commence your morning exercise routine, is it not the case that rainfall persists consistently? If you resonate with this sentiment, then meditation presents no disparity.

While engaged in the act of meditation, it is imperative to acknowledge that obstructions can originate not solely from external sources, but also from within oneself. A sense of inadequacy, a perception of unaccomplishment, or simply a notion that one's efforts could be directed towards more significant endeavors. Although it will never be effortless, it is indeed feasible to surmount these challenges by exerting your utmost effort, thereby experiencing a transformative shift in your life through the regular practice of meditation.

Herein lies a compendium of the prevailing impediments to the practice of meditation:

Experiencing a lack of available time

The primary impediment to engaging in meditation is a prevailing sense of insufficiency in terms of available time. However, it remains an undeniable reality that time is always insufficient to engage in even the most crucial pursuits in life. It is quite amusing that you have the capacity to spend a full 30 minutes engaged in idleness, yet you console yourself under the presumption of relaxation. When consulting the most advanced practitioners of meditation, one discerns that prior to embarking on their meditation journey, they had diligently prepared to commence this practice for an extended period of time.

To ascertain whether time can be considered a justifiable pretext, it is imperative to undertake a self-evaluation. Do you ever find yourself in moments of inactivity? Do you manage to get a full 10 hours of sleep? Do you devote a substantial amount of time to television consumption, thus leaving insufficient time for socializing with your acquaintances? Should any of the aforementioned circumstances pertain to you and if your response is affirmative, it can be regarded as a hindrance.

Occasionally, one may find oneself engrossed in such busyness that the luxury of acquiring even a spare minute becomes scarce. In this particular instance, I implore you to persevere in pursuing your aspiration of engaging in meditation. Acquire the skill of practicing meditation during the act of showering, when in a state of waiting for public transportation, or even during the process of commuting. In the event that you are constrained by time constraints, make the most of any available opportunity to engage in the practice of meditation.

Falling asleep

I understand that you may find this concept unfamiliar or peculiar if you have not previously encountered it. Are you aware that there exist individuals who, upon initiating a meditation practice, unexpectedly succumb to unconscious sleep within a few minutes? It becomes challenging to maintain a meditation session, even for five minutes, despite having obtained an ample amount of sleep. According to meditation instructors, the resolution lies within one's consciousness. This issue is frequently encountered by beginners, but as you advance, your ability to sustain your session will improve.

Distractions

Meditation is commonly characterized by maintaining a state of calmness and focused contemplation on a single idea or subject. Nevertheless, this task proves to be quite challenging. Achieving a state of mental relaxation and maintaining focus on a singular thought is a challenging endeavor. For instance, in the event that one finds oneself caught in a traffic congestion, engaging in the practice of meditation proves to be the most prudent course of action. Adopt a relaxed posture, release all thoughts from your mind, and direct your sole attention towards regulating your breath. This might not function seamlessly for a significant portion of our group. The rationale behind this is the presence of multiple thoughts concurrently traversing your mind. If an individual is enroute to a workplace, concerns may arise regarding unmet deadlines, potential tardiness, or the workload they will encounter throughout the day. This will create challenges for your ability to attain mental relaxation and concentration.

Bear in mind that the purpose of meditation is to enable you to confront the emerging challenges and issues within your mind. Thus, in instances when these interferences impede your meditation, it becomes challenging to resolve them through the practice of meditation.

Great anticipation from the onset.

An additional hindrance that carries greater significance when individuals perceive a lack of time is the inclination to anticipate instantaneous outcomes. Meditation does not possess a magical quality that guarantees the immediate manifestation of its benefits the very next day. Occasionally, it may require a considerable amount of time before an individual perceives any singular advantage. There is no greater displeasure than an individual who demands instant outcomes without having attained proficiency in the practice of meditation. In order to overcome this impediment, it is necessary for individuals to appropriately align their expectations and gain a comprehensive understanding of the procedural aspects involved. Acquiring knowledge about the process enables the practitioner to discern instances of incorrect meditation and effectively assess the outcomes.

Mediation Myths

This particular impediment is frequently observed among individuals who have not yet commenced their meditation practice. There exist individuals who hold the belief that meditation is interconnected with a specific faith. This evokes a sense of apprehension among them, as though engaging in meditation would be regarded as a violation of their religious beliefs. Nonetheless, these myths are devoid of veracity. In contemporary times, meditation transcends all religious boundaries. A mere fraction of the global population engages in meditation for spiritual purposes, while the majority practice it to attain various other advantages.

Restlessness and boredom

Some individuals perceive meditation as unconventional or eccentric. By maintaining composure and actively pursuing personal growth, how can one effectively embark on a transformative journey? Others find it difficult to remain still or acquire mastery of the meditation technique.

Some individuals assert that they find the act of simply sitting down to be tedious. Additionally, it poses a significant difficulty for individuals who perceive meditation as a means of enhancing concentration, inducing relaxation, or aiding in the cultivation of focus. In order to surmount this challenge, individuals must acquire a comprehensive understanding of the underlying principles and mechanics of meditation, thereby enabling them to cultivate mental discipline and foster a genuine enthusiasm.

The path towards attaining a state of meditation is always challenging and will remain so. However, there is invariably an available solution. If one maintains unwavering determination, they will acquire the ability to surmount any impediment presented in their path. The most effective strategy for surmounting these obstacles is perceiving them as chances to transcend your capabilities and emerge in an even more enhanced state. When embarking upon the practice of meditation, it is essential to maintain a positive mindset and remain open to the unexpected nature of the journey ahead. One of the most remarkable aspects of engaging in meditation is that once you begin experiencing the positive outcomes, no external factors can dampen your spirits.

Choosing A Mantra

If one is at ease with the profound or transcendental connotations associated with them, it is advisable to engage in meditation with the sacred incantation of om (aum) or consider using any of the subsequent alternatives:

- Om Namah Shivaya, an ancient and widely recognized Indian mantra that carries the profound essence of humbly paying reverence to Lord Shiva or, metaphorically, acknowledging and showing respect to one's own inner self — as Shiva symbolizes the inherent divinity within all sentient beings.
- "Om mani padme hum," which means "the jewel in the lotus" in literal translation, is a widely recognized and esteemed mantra that holds great significance among Tibetan Buddhists.
- "La ilaha illa'llah" is a phrase derived from the Koran and commonly

employed as a sacred chant within the Sufic practice, encapsulating the profound notion that 'There exists no deity except Allah'.

- In the Christian tradition, the phrase "kyrie eleison" from Greek denotes a plea to the Lord for mercy.
- "Maranatha", an Aramaic phrase deriving from the Christian tradition, meaning "Come, Lord".
- The term "abba" is derived from Aramaic, signifying "Father" and commonly employed by members of the Jesuit order.
- Hallelujah or alleluia, originating from the Hebrew language, conveying the meaning 'exalt the divine'
- In accordance with Jewish tradition, the phrase "ANoKhY, I am" is utilized.

If you desire to employ a spiritual mantra, yet find yourself discomfited with any of the aforementioned options, you may opt for a name of the Divine or an uplifting phrase derived from a sacred text, while ensuring it is of a moderate length. A group of devout Christians employ the subsequent phrases as recitations:

Remain calm and recognize that I am the Almighty

O Lord Jesus Christ, the divine offspring, I beseech you to bestow your mercy upon me.
Alternatively, this prayer may also be employed in a more concise manner: "
"Lord Jesus Christ" - uttered during the act of inspiration
"I humbly implore your compassion" - as I release my breath

If you have a preference for employing a neutral or ambiguous mantra, feel free to select any auditory or lexical entity that resonates with you, with a preference for brevity. Alternatively, if you believe that a mantra devoid of religious or mystical connotations would be more beneficial for you, you may opt to employ expressions and terms that evoke positivity, such as 'reside in the present moment', 'affection', 'tranquility', or 'unity'. Certain individuals effectively utilize their own name as a form of meditative mantra.

Once you have established a mantra that resonates positively with you, adhere to it consistently. The continuous repetition of the same mantra not only enhances its efficacy but also equips you with a valuable technique to invoke serenity or direct your concentration amidst the chaos and challenges of everyday existence.

Methods for Practicing Mantra Meditation

Please assume a relaxed and vertical posture, either by sitting on the floor or on a chair, or by reclining. Please shut your eyes and adopt a state of relaxation. Inhale and exhale in a calm and effortless manner, while consciously and silently reciting your selected mantra at a pace akin to ordinary speech. Should you desire, it is possible for you to recite the mantra in alignment with the cadence of your breath, either once or twice during the act of inhaling, and once or twice during the act of exhaling. Fully engross yourself in the mantra and be completely absorbed by its essence. Lose yourself in meditation. When utilizing a spiritual mantra, it is imperative to recite it while acknowledging and embracing the fundamental connection between oneself, the mantra, and its ultimate purpose - the inner being.

After achieving a state of tranquility, it is superfluous to continue the repetition of the mantra. There is no need for concern when thoughts and images transiently traverse your mind. Permit their entry and exit, while maintaining your concentration on the mantra. Should your focus begin to drift, kindly redirect it towards the repetition of the chosen mantra.

The technique known as the hamsa, also referred to as so'ham,

The hamsa technique, as elucidated in a classical Sanskrit manuscript on the discipline of yoga known as the Vijñānabhairava, encompasses a straightforward and intrinsic practice of attentively observing the inhalation and exhalation of breath. Inhalation is associated with the auditory perception of the sound "ha", while exhalation is correlated with the auditory perception of the sound "sah". The occurrence of the m sound is automatic at the intersection of the ha and the sah. Therefore, the utterance of hamsa resonates ceaselessly through every sentient being, regardless of their conscious recognition, thus qualifying it as a mantra. It is commonly known as the natural mantra, given that its repetition occurs effortlessly and spontaneously, without necessitating any mental or verbal recitation.

The essence of the mantra signifies the union of the individual self and the universal self, as it conveys the message of 'I am that' (signifying the individual self as 'I am' and the universal self as 'that'). When the concept of hamsa is deliberately and repeatedly reflected upon, it transforms into the realization of so'ham, signifying 'I am that'. This occurs due to the grammatical principles of Sanskrit, where the combination of sah and aham results in the formation of the conjunction so'ham. Hamsa and so'ham are therefore synonymous mantras that hold identical significance. The act of reversing the syllables effectively transfers the focus from personal awareness to a broader awareness encompassing everything.

Instructions for practicing meditation with the hamsa (so/ham) technique

Please assume a comfortable position in a tranquil environment, ensuring that your eyes are either partially or completely shut, according to the instructions provided in Chapter 3. Engage in natural respiration while directing your attention towards the auditory perception of the breath during both inhalation and exhalation, uttering the sound 'ha' on the inhalation and 'sah' (or 'so') on the exhalation. Direct your attention towards the intervals between each inhalation and exhalation - specifically, the internal pause between the phonetic sounds "ha" and "sah" that corresponds with the production of the sound "m", as well as the external space that ensues when "sah" dissipates, prior to the emergence of "ha".

Permit thoughts and mental imagery to transit through your cognitive realm, adopting a stance that allows their passage while directing your focus onto the process of respiration.

Should your focus falter, calmly redirect it towards the breath. As increments occur, the mind attains a profound state of tranquility. Nevertheless, it is crucial that you permit this process to occur autonomously, refraining from impeding the innate cadence of your respiration.

Visual meditation

Pictorial and symbolic imagery are prevalent in nearly all mystical and religious customs, serving as a catalyst for heightened spiritual consciousness. Consequently, this practice has led to the creation of extraordinary artistic masterpieces within certain traditions. In the context of the Eastern Orthodox Church, it has been a longstanding tradition to employ icons, which are commonly portrayed as paintings on small wooden panels, depicting figures such as Christ, the Virgin Mary, or various Saints. These icons serve as valuable aids in fostering and enhancing devotional practices. Mystical diagrams hold significant value as a supplementary tool for meditation in Eastern cultures, specifically within specific Buddhist and Hindu practices. It is likely that these diagrams have attained their most comprehensive manifestation and utmost intricacy within the illustrious realm of tantric yoga, through the utilization of vibrant hues, intricate imagery, and profound symbolism. The aforementioned diagrams, explicated further in the subsequent analysis, establish the foundation for contemplation in the tantric disciple, meticulously crafted to redirect focus inward and bolster the progress of spiritual advancement.

However, it is not imperative to engage with images of such intricate complexity. Instead, individuals who are new to the practice of visual meditation are advised to commence by focusing their attention on, and subsequently conjuring mental imagery of, a modest, unremarkable object. As the ability to visualize advances, one can gradually strive for more intricate and intricate images. Illuminating a candle within a room devoid of light represents a straightforward method to commence an activity. A fire inherently captures one's attention, akin to how a hearth serves as an inherent central element in a space, making it effortless to sustain a vivid mental image. The act of engaging in visual meditation commences with fixating one's gaze upon the selected object or symbol. Subsequently, the eyes are shut and the object is mentally visualized, with the latter being the more nuanced technique. During the initial phases of meditation, maintaining a clear, distinct mental image can prove to be rather challenging, prompting the meditator to predominantly keep their eyes open and focus on the tangible object or visual representation. With diligent application, the task of maintaining a stable mental image will gradually become more effortless, eventually rendering the reliance on the physical object unnecessary.

The form of meditation discussed in this section should not be misconstrued with the visualization technique frequently employed in therapeutic settings or as a means to enhance self-healing and personal development. This alternative form of visualization typically hinges upon a guided formulation of fantasies, aimed at offering the visualizer or therapist a deeper understanding of character or personal issues. Alternatively, it may entail a sequence of constructive assertions, among other techniques. In this scenario, a conscious cognitive process is unfolding, whereas the type of meditation elucidated in this literary work strives to achieve mental tranquility and the cessation of thoughts, employing various methods that facilitate the achievement of this state devoid of cogitation. The intent behind engaging in the act of observing and mentally reconstructing an object is to direct and concentrate one's attention. The objective is to maintain an awareness of the subject without engaging in creative or rational thought processes, or engaging in free association. The practitioner encounters the object on an experiential level instead of contemplating it intellectually, fully immersing themselves in it and merging with it.

An alternative method of visualization employed in certain meditation practices entails the generation of elaborate cognitive constructs solely through the power of imagination. This type of meditation is exemplified in the tantric mysticism practiced in Tibet, where practitioners employ an advanced technique of mentally manifesting deities and subsequently merging their consciousness with these divine beings, embodying their inherent attributes and characteristics. Such visualizations lie outside the purview of this book and should be undertaken solely under the supervision of a trustworthy instructor.

Selecting a visual artifact or depiction

As previously stated, employing a illuminated candle or another source of light juxtaposed against a dark backdrop serves as an optimal means of capturing the attention of novices. However, it is also possible to utilize a straightforward item or visual representation, preferably one that is visually appealing and carries neutral connotations. Elements from nature are frequently selected, such as a bloom, a strand of foliage, or a pebble. Geometric forms, including spheres, as well as shades, can be employed with remarkable efficacy.

The Visuddhimagga, a Buddhist text from the fourth century, delineates ten diverse kasinas, or objects of visual meditation, as elaborated upon in the kasina meditations. These elements encompass the following: earth, air, fire, and water; the colors blue, yellow, red, and white; as well as light and space. In order to engage in contemplation of a specific elemental aspect, the practitioner directs their attention towards a suitable entity, for instance, a receptacle containing soil, an assemblage resembling the boughs of a tree swaying with the breeze, a flickering flame, or a vessel brimming with water. In contemplation of a single hue, the practitioner directs their gaze toward any object exhibiting the corresponding color. This could be an ordinary piece of paper or a painted disc in the selected hue, or it could manifest as a flower displaying the desired color, a leaf, a cushion, and similar options. One can engage in the practice of meditating on light by focusing one's attention on a concentrated area of illumination created by a spotlight, the refraction of light upon the surface of water, or the gentle beams permeating through lush foliage. A vacant receptacle or the interstitial areas amidst objects could effectively assume the role of focal point for the practice of meditation on spatiality.

Mystic and religious symbols

Mystical and religious doctrines present an abundant repertoire of content that can be employed as reservoirs for contemplative imagery. The most widely recognized religious icon in the Western hemisphere is the Cross, which serves as the emblem of the Christian faith. An additional emblem that bears recognition from numerous individuals is the Buddhist Wheel of Life or Becoming, exemplifying, to some extent, the recurring pattern of life and the deceptive essence of the world in terms of sensory perception. Furthermore, it can be perceived as a cognitive blueprint of the human psyche.

Another example is the Chinese yin-yang symbol, which exemplifies the inception of the cosmos - the realm of shapes and entities - from i'ai chi, the celestial energy or ultimate truth that exists in its pure, undifferentiated, and shapeless state. The circular symbol, which serves as the representation of t'ai chi, is meticulously divided into two distinct sections, namely yin (the visually darker region) and yang (the visually lighter region). The concepts of yin and yang symbolize the opposing yet complementary aspects of t'ai chi, indicating the various dichotomies that exist within nature and human existence - such as femininity and masculinity, nocturnal and diurnal, passivity and activity, lunar and solar, among others. However, each one encompasses the inherent essence of the other, exemplified by the minuscule spheres depicted in the illustration.

In the realm of Jewish mysticism, the Tree of Life emerges as a significant embodiment. It assumes the form of a graphical depiction that elucidates the ten celestial powers, also known as Sefirot, responsible for the genesis and preservation of the material cosmos.

These energies are additionally believed to align with specific bodily locations, similar to the chakras within the yoga framework.

What Hypnosis Is And What It Is Not And What Benefits It Has On Insomnia Disorder

What Does Hypnosis Entail?

Hypnosis can be described as a cognitive condition akin to a trance, characterized by heightened attentiveness, focus, and susceptibility to suggestions. Hypnosis is frequently characterized not as a state akin to sleep, but instead as an enhanced state of focused attention and suggestibility, accompanied by vivid imaginative experiences. Individuals frequently experience drowsiness and appear to be in a trance-like condition, yet they possess heightened sensitivity to their surroundings.

Hypnosis serves as a direct and uncomplicated method utilized for therapeutic purposes, notwithstanding the prevalence of numerous misconceptions and misinterpretations. The medical and therapeutic advantages of hypnosis have been substantiated, particularly in the realm of pain and anxiety alleviation. Hypnosis has also been proposed as a potential means of mitigating symptoms associated with dementia.

The phenomenon of hypnotic trance states has a history that spans thousands of years, with the practice of hypnosis gaining prominence during the latter half of the 18th century under the influence of renowned physician Franz Mesmer. Due to Mesmer's enigmatic perspectives, the initial implementation of the practice faced challenges. However, over time, the intrigue surrounding it transitioned into a more empirical and scholarly engagement.

The hypnotist assists in inducing relaxation and composure in order to facilitate greater receptiveness to suggestions. The phenomenon of being entranced by daydreaming can be likened to hypnosis. If one aspires for a specific outcome to materialize, it is customary to selectively suppress any divergent thoughts or distractions and devote singular attention towards realizing this envisioned outcome. During the state of hypnosis, individuals are similarly predisposed to wholeheartedly focus on the present experience, undeterred by extraneous thoughts or auditory stimuli.

Various maladies, disorders, and grievances can be effectively addressed through the employment of hypnosis. As an example, the facilitation of suggestibility through hypnosis can be beneficial in alleviating symptoms of anxiety or depression. Hypnotic therapy is also employed as a means of addressing specific medical ailments, including disturbances in the gastrointestinal system, dermatological conditions, and chronic pain. Nevertheless, not all interventions are proactive in nature. Furthermore, scholars have employed hypnosis as a means to acquire knowledge pertaining to its impact on cognition, recollection, sensory experience, and the interpretation of stimuli.

Shall we examine a few illustrations to enhance our comprehension of the mechanics of hypnosis? Consider the act of biting your nails and the undesirable habit you wish to eliminate. Arrange a meeting with a hypnotist for this objective. The hypnotist kindly requests that you designate a seating or reclining location upon entering the room. You shall assume a position of seated repose, whereupon the hypnotist shall inquire as to your intended course of action. Therefore, the hypnotist is requesting that you gently shut your eyes and create a mental image of yourself occupying your preferred location, such as a tranquil beach or a serene hilltop. The hypnotist guides you through a sequence of perspectives to induce a state of relaxation and tranquility. The hypnotist asserts that there is no longer a necessity for you to engage in nail-biting behavior once you are in a state of ease. He instructs you, with a polished and meticulous appearance, to envision the hairstyle. That concept would exert a disproportionately profound impact on your cognitive faculties within the context of your heightened state of tranquility, surpassing its potential influence in any other circumstance. A composed and self-assured mindset renders you highly receptive. Once the envisioned mental image has been generated, the hypnotist employs a specific utterance such as 'subsequently, it becomes appropriate to reestablish focus on the present' in order to guide the individual into resuming their awareness by opening their eyes.

During the late 19th century, hypnotism gained popularity within the domain of mental disorder treatment and was specifically implemented in the context of hysteria among women, as elucidated by Jean-Martin Charcot. This particular work served as a source of inspiration for Sigmund Freud, thereby significantly influencing the development of his psychoanalytic theory.

Within the most recent timeframe, a multitude of diverse theories have emerged in order to explicate the mechanisms underlying the phenomenon of hypnosis. Hilgard's theory of hypnosis, known as neodissociation theory, is widely recognized as one of the most prominent ideas in the field.

As per Hilgard's findings, during a state of hypnosis, a split consciousness is experienced by two distinct streams of mental activity. While one aspect of awareness responds to the hypnotist's suggestions, there exists another detached aspect that comprehends information extending beyond the conscious state of the hypnotized individual.

For over two centuries, individuals have engaged in contemplation and discourse regarding the phenomenon of hypnosis; nevertheless, the scientific community has not achieved a comprehensive understanding of its underlying mechanisms. The actions exhibited by individuals during hypnosis are observable, however, the underlying motives driving these actions remain obscure. This puzzle represents a fractional component within a larger jigsaw puzzle: the intricacies of cognitive processes. In brief, it is uncertain whether scientists can attain a conclusive comprehension of the mind, thereby leaving the phenomenon of effective hypnosis for gambling purposes shrouded in enigma.

However, psychologists possess a comprehensive understanding of the fundamental aspects of hypnosis and have formulated a detailed account regarding its mechanisms of operation. It encompasses a state of deep trance, characterized by heightened suggestibility, profound relaxation, and enhanced creative capacity. It diverges from the state of sleep, as the subject remains continuously vigilant. The sensation of becoming completely absorbed by a literary work or film is frequently likened to, if not surpassed by, the act of daydreaming. You are fully aware and capable of enduring a significant amount of external stimuli. You devote considerable attention to the subject, virtually disregarding any other cognitive processes.

Individuals experience a sense of liberation and self-assurance within this particular cognitive state. This is likely due to the fact that they address the concerns and doubts that typically govern their actions. While engrossed in your narrative, concerns pertaining to your professional pursuits, familial obligations, and other matters gradually recede, leaving only the subject of your story to occupy your thoughts entirely within the realm of the screen. You will experience an equivalent sensation while engaging in a film.

In this particular instance, you display a high susceptibility to influence. Namely, it is highly likely that you will wholeheartedly embrace the notion as soon as the hypnotist instructs you to perform a particular action. That is precisely what imbues stage hypnotists with a sense of excitement. Individuals with heightened sensitivity tend to exhibit reserved behaviors, yet they may abruptly embark on a journey across the stage while firmly grasping or passionately vocalizing at full volume. The apprehension regarding perplexity seems to be diminishing in the public sphere. However, even with continuous practice, the individual's perception of security and morality remains steadfastly ingrained. It is not possible to coerce a hypnotist into making you do something against your will.

The critical approach to hypnosis involves the direct access to an individual's unconscious mind. Typically, within one's conscious state, one is primarily cognizant of cognitive processes. One is cognizant of the challenges at hand, carefully selects words while communicating, and makes a conscious effort to remember the location of their keys.

Your subconscious mind possesses an innate ability to effortlessly oversee all your endeavors. You are not consciously engaging in minute-by-minute implementation of the respiratory techniques, as it is the subconscious mind that controls this process. One does not consciously consider every minute action performed while operating a motor vehicle; numerous minor actions are constructed within the depths of one's subconscious mind. The sensory information acquired by the body is also processed by the subconscious mind.

In summary, the veritable instigator responsible for the surgical procedure is your subconscious intellect, as it orchestrates a substantial portion of cognitive processes and exerts significant influence in determining your actions. During wakefulness, your conscious mind operates to examine these thoughts, render judgments, and implement certain concepts. Furthermore, it facilitates the processing and transmission of novel information to the subconscious realm. Nevertheless, during sleep, the conscious mind recedes, allowing the unconscious to exert unrestrained influence.

Psychiatrists propose that the induction of profound relaxation and dedicated hypnosis training helps to alleviate cognitive engagement and reduce conscious involvement in one's thought processes. You possess knowledge of the current events in this state, although your conscious awareness has receded to the background in deference to your subconscious mind. Fundamentally, you and the hypnotist will establish direct communication with the subconscious mind. During the process of hypnotism, it seems as if your brain accesses a control panel, so to speak.

Furthermore, we also explored the notion that the conscious mind should assume a subordinate role during hypnosis, allowing for a direct and uninhibited interaction between yourself and the hypnotist. This theory has been widely embraced by the psychiatric community due to its capacity to effectively elucidate the fundamental characteristics of the hypnotic state.

The rationale behind the lightheartedness and lack of self-restraint exhibited by individuals under hypnosis holds particular significance. The conscious mind serves as the primary restraining factor in your creative process, as it is tasked with exercising caution. Conversely, the subconscious mind acts as a realm of boundless imagination and innate drive. One experiences heightened liberty and enhanced creativity in the presence of a subconscious mind that governs their actions. Your conscious mind must not impede all.

This theory posits that individuals under hypnosis exhibit peculiar behavior due to the absence of filtration and relaying of information by the conscious mind. It appears that the hypnotist's suggestions emanate not from an external source but rather directly from the depths of the subconscious mind. You promptly address these impulses and suggestions, much in the same manner as you handle your own thoughts. It is inherent that your subconscious bears awareness, an innate drive for self-preservation, and a multitude of thoughts that it may not concur with.

The subconscious governs bodily sensations encompassing taste, touch, sight, and emotion. Assuming that the entrance door is ajar, the hypnotist shall establish direct communication with your subconscious mind. In such an instance, it is feasible to evoke all of these emotions, thereby allowing you to experience the sensation akin to that of enjoying a milkshake cake while also experiencing contentment, fulfillment, and various other sentiments.

Furthermore, the unconscious mind serves as the repository of your memories. Through the use of hypnosis, individuals are able to regain access to past events that were previously completely forgotten, while psychiatrists can employ hypnotherapy to intentionally induce the recollection of a memory in order to ultimately address a related personal issue. Due to the demonstrable state of the subject's mind, it is possible for false recollections to be constructed. Consequently, psychiatrists must exercise utmost caution when delving into the historical aspects of a hypnotic subject.

The basis of this hypnosis theory primarily rests on logical deduction, albeit with additional backing from certain physiological evidence. In the upcoming segment, we will examine the physical data scrutinized by investigators employing hypnosis.

Multiple studies have sought to compare the somatic manifestations exhibited by individuals under hypnotic conditions to those demonstrated by non-hypnotized individuals. In the majority of these experiments, there was no discernible physical change associated with the hypnotic trance state. The individual's cardiac and pulmonary parameters may exhibit a decline, which should not be attributed solely to the hypnotic state, as it can be attributed to the inherent relaxation experienced during the hypnotic procedure.

Insights from Rogers and Maslow Regarding the Concept of Humanism

The advent of the 20th century signified the ascendency of psychoanalysis and behaviorism as the prevailing forces shaping American psychology. Nevertheless, certain scholars have identified constraints within the current psychology frameworks, despite their significant influence within the discipline. Their primary objections lay in the inherent tendency of behaviorism to oversimplify, its deterministic outlook, and its propensity for pessimism. Behaviorism was also regarded as possessing deterministic characteristics, as it focused exclusively on human conduct, which is determined by a combination of genetic factors and environmental influences.

Certain psychologists began to shift their focus towards intentionality, personal agency, and a positive orientation towards behavior and self-perception. It was through this paradigm shift that the field of humanism emerged. Humanism refers to a psychological framework that accentuates the inherent capacity for benevolence present in every individual. Abraham Maslow and Carl Rogers emerge as prominent proponents of the humanistic perspective.

Abraham Maslow is renowned for his classification of human needs within a hierarchical framework, commencing with the most fundamental necessities such as sustenance, hydration, and habitation, and culminating at the apex of the hierarchy with the pursuit of self-actualization. In his view, the needs serve as crucial incentives for behavior until an individual attains maximum potential. This hierarchy centered its attention on the favorable attributes of the human being.

Carl Rogers, an American psychologist, similarly underscored the notion that inherent goodness resides within individuals, mirroring the perspective espoused by Maslow. He conducted his research by employing a therapeutic modality known as client-centered therapy, with the intention of assisting clients in managing the underlying problems that motivated them to pursue therapy. The focal point of the therapeutic sessions revolves around assigning the primary responsibility for leading the treatment process to the client. The therapist must consequently exhibit empathy, authenticity, and unwavering positive regard. Rogers believed that individuals possess a superior capacity to navigate and comprehend their own lives compared to any other party.

Collectively, humanism has exerted substantial influence in the realm of psychological research and application. The application of their methodologies, including the utilization of the client-centered approach, continues to be prevalent in contemporary therapeutic practices.

Inauguration of the Cognitive Revolution

The behavioral approach, characterized by its emphasis on observable behavior and objectivity, had temporarily redirected attention away from the realm of cognition. On the other hand, proponents of humanism shifted the emphasis towards the individual, recognizing their capacity for introspection and self-awareness. Nevertheless, in the 1950s, advancements in computer science, neuroscience, and linguistics redirected the focus towards the mind, marking the onset of a conceptual shift known as the cognitive revolution.

The revolution additionally fostered a discourse between European and American psychologists, who had not previously engaged in substantial interaction. Psychologists have also engaged in collaborations with linguists, computer scientists, anthropologists, neuroscientists, and experts from various disciplines. The nomenclature cognitive sciences was bestowed upon this interdisciplinary collaboration, which continues to exert significant influence within contemporary psychology.

Thought

The diverse and complex nature of our thoughts can be truly captivating. Cognition is an elevated cognitive process accountable for rationality, decision-making, unconventional thinking, innovative thinking, and analytical reasoning. To facilitate this process, the brain generates concepts by utilizing ideas, individuals, entities, and assorted elements that spring forth within one's thoughts.

Generally, this is intended to optimize your cognitive functioning. Nevertheless, there are instances in which an individual demonstrates rationality, while at other times, they exhibit irrationality. On occasion, individuals may opt for expeditious methods to expedite the processing of information, disregarding the crucial elements. Frequently, this gives rise to cognitive bias, whereby thoughts deviate from the standard process of reasoning and are instead inclined towards a singular idea. One instance illustrating this concept is observed in gambling, wherein an individual believes they possess the ability to precisely forecast a given outcome.

Cognitive bias can sometimes give rise to cognitive distortions that are highly irrational and pessimistic in nature. For instance, an individual may perceive, "I lack the capability to provide for myself," to imply that the person believes they are unable to generate sufficient income to sustain their own well-being. This statement fails to take into account the potential scenario where an individual can successfully secure a desirable employment opportunity through their own efforts.

It is imperative to bear in mind that one has the capacity to alter such thoughts, thereby cultivating more constructive and optimistic ones. If you find yourself overwhelmed by negativity, it is advisable to confide in someone about your feelings.

Intelligence

Intelligence facilitates the decision-making process by amalgamating multiple sources of information prior to reaching a conclusion, thereby ensuring that the decision made is well-informed. There exist various forms of intellect, encompassing musical intelligence, intrapersonal intelligence, logical-mathematical intelligence, linguistic intelligence, and a range of other advanced cognitive faculties. The concept of emotional intelligence has garnered significant interest due to its capacity to facilitate individuals in effectively navigating their emotions and effectively overcoming the hurdles they encounter.

Language

Human individuals possess the capability to grasp and generate diverse lexicons and phonetics, amalgamating alphabets to formulate sentences, and effectively conveying their thoughts and sentiments. Furthermore, the aspect of nonverbal communication, which encompasses body language, is occasionally encompassed in this context as well.

Language evolves over the course of an individual's lifespan, and the aptitude for effective communication varies substantially among individuals. Nevertheless, it should be noted that all of these skills can be acquired through education and experience, indicating that individuals have the potential to enhance their abilities through dedicated practice. An individual afflicted with language disorders may encounter challenges in effectively communicating, but through therapeutic intervention, they can acquire enhanced communication skills or discover alternative means of conveying their thoughts and ideas. The cognitive processes associated with language play a crucial role in facilitating the individual's acquisition of effective communication skills.

Enhancing Your Cognitive Functions

Irrespective of one's age and level of experience, there is perpetually a potential for individuals to engage in training and enhancing their cognitive faculties. Herein, we present a number of guidelines to assist you in achieving this objective.

Maintain good health

The interconnectedness of your mental and physical health is paramount, as this synergy ultimately dictates the efficiency of your cognitive faculties. The acquisition of unfavorable behaviors during one's journey can detrimentally impact one's cognitive abilities and subsequently have repercussions on one's performance in multiple facets of life.

Excessive consumption of alcohol or any other psychoactive substance is likely to impair cognitive functions and impede one's capacity to make rational judgments. Certain individuals may experience a loss of self-regulation and emotional mastery. Continuous engagement with your mobile device, to the exclusion of other activities, will result in the disregard of your interpersonal connections, the neglect of your well-being and physical condition, as well as the deterioration of your dietary habits. By doing so, you will be disregarding your mental well-being, thus impacting your cognitive functioning. Do not be taken aback if individuals commence to assert that you are becoming disconnected from the realm of actuality.

Leverage technology to your advantage. Whilst the potential to develop detrimental habits resulting from excessive technology use exists, such as the manifestation of phone addiction, there are viable measures one can undertake on a daily basis to enhance cognitive function in an effortless and enjoyable manner.

Currently, there exists a form of cognitive enhancement known as brain training, which encompasses engaging games and activities that can be undertaken to bolster and restore certain cognitive functions such as strategic thinking, recollection, mental flexibility, and perceptual exploration. These activities cater to individuals of both juvenile and mature age groups. Additionally, a comparative analysis of the outcomes obtained from these activities vis-à-vis those of other individuals can be pursued, thereby augmenting the overall intrigue.

Develop strong analytical skills and cultivate a discerning mindset

Acquire the skill of self-inquiry and engage in critical thinking by formulating inquiries and generating potential counterarguments in response. Engaging in this activity facilitates the cultivation of critical thinking skills, fostering an awareness that concurrent enhancements in creativity, reasoning, and language aptitude are also achievable. An inquisitive nature should prompt you to interrogate all that surrounds you.

Become a reader
Engaging in literary pursuits enhances one's comprehension and awareness of various subjects. Furthermore, aside from the gratification it induces, it prompts one to interrogate the existing state of affairs. One starts contemplating alternative approaches that could have been employed, taking into account the newly acquired understanding of the situation. Engaging in literature offers a valuable chance to enhance one's linguistic proficiency and aptitude for effective communication.

Contemplate the advancements you have achieved.

Personal evaluations are of utmost importance as they enable individuals to assess their current performance in relation to their past accomplishments. Through self-evaluation, individuals gain a profound understanding of their achievements and recognize the realms in which they should focus on enhancing to sustain their progression. It is imperative that you maintain faith in your own capabilities and have confidence in your potential to enhance your cognitive faculties. Ultimately, you will acquire the skill of maintaining consistency and enhancing your self-assurance.

Allocate time for engaging in artistic endeavors.

Engage in pursuits and pastimes that foster expressions of creativity. This may manifest itself through the composition of songs and narratives, the art of dancing, or any other endeavor that you desire to undertake. The cultivation of artistic ingenuity fosters resilience by conscientiously engaging in repetitive practice until a state of proficiency is attained. Furthermore, it enhances your capacity to focus, intellect, prowess in finding solutions, as well as aiding in the attainment of a state of tranquility and stress relief.

Do not undertake excessive quantities concurrently.

We are burdened with numerous responsibilities, and frequently find ourselves caught in the frenzy of prioritizing our tasks. Several individuals may feel inclined to divert their attention towards multiple tasks simultaneously. Nevertheless, engaging in multitasking may prove to be unproductive as it divides your focus across multiple activities. As an illustration, in the event of opting to compose your assignment while concurrently viewing a film, it is conceivable that focus may become compromised for both activities at some juncture. If you simultaneously engage in the task of laundering while preparing a meal, there is a high probability that both endeavors will not be executed flawlessly. It is imperative that you direct your attention to one project at a time, with the intention of deriving satisfaction from the process and enhancing your overall efficiency. In addition, you circumvent procrastination by virtue of concentrating on a single task, rendering it increasingly arduous for potential distractions to divert your attention.

Educate and cultivate children's abilities to effectively resolve challenges "

While it is imperative to offer assistance and guidance to children, it is equally important to instill in them a sense of independence and resilience. Addressing and resolving issues will foster the development of their cognitive abilities and enhance their intellectual faculties, commencing from an early stage.

Embrace The Present Moment While Engaging In The Practice Of Meditation.

In addition to the customary practice of seated meditation, there exist alternative approaches and methods that can enhance your meditation routine, enabling you to attain mental tranquility and fully savor the present moment. Presented herein are several suggestions on methods to cultivate mental tranquility and embrace the present moment.

1. Engage in the activity of walking meditation—An integration of physical movement and the practice of mindfulness meditation. During the practice of walking meditation, one directs their attention towards the inhalation and exhalation of breath, as

well as the movements of their steps, interspersed with periodic moments of observing and acknowledging the surrounding scenery with a sense of appreciation. The practice of walking meditation proves to be highly efficacious in alleviating mental clutter and anxieties. It facilitates one's ability to be present in the current moment.

2. Engage in introspection and establish a connection with your thoughts – Often, we passively allow our thoughts to come and go, without consciously acknowledging their presence. Consequently, your mind becomes inundated with concerns and negative thought patterns. Please exercise caution in regard to your thoughts. Designate a specific period within your daily schedule during which you engage in the activity of sitting down and devoting your attention solely to your breath,

while diligently implementing the fundamental mindfulness methods that we have previously covered in the preceding sections. Ensure that you consciously recognize every thought that arises in your mind without forming judgments, and subsequently redirect your attention to your breath.

3. Engage in Mindful Rest – Daily, within the confines of your professional or educational environment, allocate moments to still your thoughts and allow your mind to unwind and recuperate. Allocate a portion of your coffee break to either engage in a period of tranquil contemplation at your workstation or embark on a brief stroll within the vicinity of the local area.

4. Cease cerebral activity - an increasingly refined method to cultivate mental stillness involves purging the

mind of all thoughts. Therefore, it is necessary to halt the inception of a thought prior to its entrance into the cognitive realm. Furthermore, it implies the necessity of consistently monitoring and filtering one's thoughts in order to prevent them from exerting undue influence over one's actions and behaviors. This method is exclusive to individuals who have attained exceptional psychological resilience through the consistent implementation of meditation in their everyday routine.

Do not exist as though you are merely meandering through existence. Avoid fixating on past events or excessively fretting over future uncertainties. By attaining mental silence, one can fully savor the present instant.

Happiness

Joy comes from embracing the present and relishing the sensation of being fully alive. That is the fundamental level of simplicity that can be achieved. If one requires modest assistance from the practice of meditation to cultivate a positive outlook on existence, there exist two uncomplicated methodologies that can be employed.

Happiness In The Moment

This straightforward meditation technique can be practiced at any given moment to cultivate a sense of well-being. It entails deriving enjoyment from the small joys that life offers.

The initial phase involves selecting a singular pleasurable activity that is typically underappreciated. A few instances could include the act of preparing and consuming an evening meal, strolling amidst nature's greenery, indulging in a warm cup of coffee, immersing oneself in a luxuriously heated bathtub filled with scented bubbles, and engaging in playful interactions with one's beloved companion animal.

Subsequently, it would be advisable to derive satisfaction from engaging in this activity and granting your senses the opportunity to fully appreciate the indulgence. Develop an understanding of the affirmative emotions that accompany engagement in the activity, including serenity, pleasure, and affection.

That's it. Such is the ease with which one can experience happiness. Ensure that you consistently engage in this practice daily for a duration of approximately one week, thereafter reflecting upon your overall emotional state resultant from the accumulated experience. Does it instill a greater sense of comfort and optimism within you?

Experiencing Contentment

Prior to retiring for the night, take a moment to contemplate the day's occurrences. Did you focus predominantly on the positives or the negatives? Have you directed your attention towards your accomplishments or setbacks? The veracity of the matter is that you possess the capability to exert influence on your mentality. Successful and content individuals consciously opt for happiness and fulfillment. When confronted with failure, they perceive it as an individual incident, separate from their identity.

In order to cultivate this mindset, you may wish to observe the following contemplative practice:

Please take a seat in a comfortable position and engage in deep respiratory exercises. Please reflect upon the joyous occasions that transpired within the past 24 hours as you continue to engage in the act of respiration. It has the potential to be a heartfelt occasion shared between a companion or a member of one's family. It has the potential to be a delectable culinary experience, an impactful short film that ignites inspiration, or a joyful and lighthearted interaction with your canine companion. Revisit the complete sequence of events mentally and luxuriate in the positive emotions it evokes.

Allow a profound sense of satisfaction and appreciation to envelop you as you reflect upon these remarkable encounters that have enriched your existence. In cases where the identification of these emotions proves challenging, direct your attention towards your heart and allow access to the sensations elicited when one is bestowed with affection and concern.

Further develop these emotions by contemplating the abundance of joyous experiences throughout the course of your life. It is important to remember to maintain a consistent practice of deep breathing.

In instances where unpleasant memories arise, envision their presence passing by akin to drifting clouds. Retain solely the positive memories. Feel free to dwell in these cherished memories for as long as you please.

This straightforward exercise is ideally performed prior to your bedtime. It promptly induces feelings of happiness while concurrently aiding in the alleviation of physical discomfort and fatigue, thus facilitating a rejuvenating night of rest.

Exercise

On numerous occasions, have you found yourself engaged in repetitive scrolling on your mobile device and experiencing a fleeting thought akin to "I desire to possess such physical appearance," subsequently followed by a somber exhalation, only to resume your scrolling unhappily? Social media has likely emerged as a significant catalyst for detrimental impacts on both self-esteem and body image. Daily, mobile phone screens exhibit videos and images of impeccably attractive individuals, garnering numerous likes and comments, thereby instilling within the viewer a sense of self-doubt and negativity.

Fashion icons and influencers such as the Kardashians have seemingly established a benchmark for women's physical aesthetics that is perceived as an exceedingly unattainable hourglass figure. Male individuals are similarly inundated with visual representations of athletes and personal trainers displaying exceedingly low levels of body fat, along with highly sculpted abdominal muscles. Social media perpetuates the notion that these body images can be attained by utilizing waist-cinching techniques, consuming herbal beverages, and consuming significant quantities of protein shakes.

What social media fails to disclose are the extensive usage of makeup, photo editing techniques, optimal lighting setups, and carefully crafted poses that are employed to create the images shared by these influencers on digital platforms. They are exceedingly impractical, yet regrettably, there exists within us a desire to perceive these idealized body images as attainable. Social media, in addition, does not promote the acceptance of cellulite, stretch marks, and body diversity.

It is becoming progressively challenging to embrace and appreciate one's physical form amidst the incessant exposure to portrayals of individuals who possess impeccable attributes. In actuality, there exists substantial variation among individual physical constitutions. Certain individuals possess a slender physique, while others exhibit a more rounded figure. Furthermore, variations in height also exist, encompassing individuals of differing statures. The external appearance of our bodies should not be of concern; rather, the focus should be on their state of well-being. The focus should be on prioritizing one's health rather than fixating on specific physical attributes such as waist size, thigh gap, or bicep size.

While acknowledging the challenges, it is crucial to express this sentiment, despite its inherent difficulty. With increased repetition, there is a higher probability that the message will gradually be internalized. Once one has acquired the understanding that a substantial portion of the content disseminated on social media is divorced from reality, it should facilitate the commencement of the journey towards cultivating self-compassion and embracing oneself.

In the contemporary era dominated by the internet, it is exceedingly challenging to elude the omnipresence of advertisements. They are indiscriminately hurled in our vicinity, no matter where we direct our gaze. However, one viable course of action would be to engage in a thorough cleansing of one's social media presence. The content to which you subject yourself on the internet significantly influences your cognitive processes and emotional state. Examine the accounts you currently follow on your social media platforms and proceed to eliminate those that elicit unfavorable emotions or foster a negative self-perception. If perusing the images posted by a particular account causes you to view your own physique in a detrimental light or leads to feelings of self-doubt, kindly exert control by selecting the option to discontinue following said account. Seek out social media accounts that promote self-esteem, body acceptance, and the embracing of all body types instead. Upon eliminating detrimental influences on social media, you will gradually observe a shift towards a less adverse body image.

A sound physique corresponds to a sound intellect.

What is the reason behind my disclosure of this information and how does it relate to the practice of mindfulness and meditation? In essence, it can be stated that a sound physical state corresponds to a sound mental state. You may choose to express your disbelief through eye-rolling; however, regardless of your personal preference, it remains an indisputable fact.

Think about it. Our physiologies are fundamentally engineered as impeccably functioning mechanisms. Consequently, if our physiques lack the appropriate motion or fail to receive the necessary sustenance to facilitate optimal performance, how can one anticipate the brain to execute its functions proficiently? I'm confident that you are familiar with the analogy between the functions of the human body and those of an automobile, involving various components required for its optimal functioning. Indeed, that analogy can be considered as one of the more effective means of elucidating the concept.

The significance of what you consume will be addressed at a later point in the book, assuming you have not opted to employ its function as a doorstop before reaching that section. In the upcoming chapter, we shall delve into the significance of initiating bodily movements as a primary focus.

Consequently, when you contemplate physical activity, what immediately comes to your thoughts? Do you entertain the mental image of Arnold Schwarzenegger's prominently tanned physique clad in a compact speedo, engaging in bicep curl exercises while effortlessly grasping an elephant in each hand? Perhaps you envision proficient yoga practitioners executing headstands at a coastal setting? Alternatively, one might consider individuals who rise at four in the morning to don a form-fitting lycra costume and engage in a jog within your local vicinity. Exercise encompasses all of these aspects; however, it is not the particular kind of exercise I will initially advocate for. So, don't panic.

Due to the progress in technology witnessed in the present century, there has been a noticeable decline in human physical activity. Various modes of transportation such as automobiles, aircraft, railways, and public transit exist, alleviating the need for individuals to exert significant physical effort to travel between destinations. Furthermore, numerous enterprises have embraced the concept of remote work, leading individuals to forego the need to depart from the solace of their personal abodes. Ever.

Although this may seem desirable, it ultimately has adverse effects on one's physical well-being. The human species, or Homosapiens, has historically engaged in vigorous pursuits as a result of evolutionary processes, encompassing activities such as animal hunting, berry gathering, and herding. Over the course of time, we persevered in our activity, diligently tending to the cultivation of fields, the production of butter, and undertaking journeys solely by foot for any necessary travels. Alternatively, one could opt for equestrian activity that requires considerable exertion, if not more.

The advent of the 21st century has significantly facilitated certain facets of existence compared to earlier times. In contemporary times, the necessity of engaging in primitive activities like wielding spears to procure sustenance has become obsolete. Instead, one can effortlessly visit a local grocery store where an extensive array of butchered and processed meat options are readily available for selection, providing utmost convenience. Are you disinclined to engage in the act of butter churning? Not an issue! The supermarket is replete with a wide variety of butter, including both salted and unsalted options. In addition to the inherent convenience, the prevalence of home-delivery services is increasing, thereby eliminating the necessity to visit physical grocery stores. Please feel free to select any items you desire, and with a single click, they will be promptly delivered to your residence.

Therefore, what prompted me to digress onto the topic of exercise and subsequently delve into the chronicles of evolutionary history? There is a underlying message to convey here: The level of physical activity in humans falls significantly short of the expected standard.

Exercise encompasses more than just push-ups, jump-squats, headstands on the beach, or bicep curls with elephants. Additionally, it involves engaging in physical activity, such as taking a leisurely stroll within the confines of your residence or garden on a regular basis or periodically performing simple exercises like reaching down to touch your toes.

It has been established that consistent physical activity can provide significant support for mental well-being. Recall the statement I made previously: a sound physical state contributes to a sound mental state. I assure you, my statement was not made in jest, nor did I simply appropriate that slogan from Pinterest. According to a research conducted by Karmel Choi, which examines the correlation between physical exercise and depression, individuals who engaged in regular fifteen-minute walks experienced a substantial reduction in depressive symptoms, with a decrease of up to 26% in their overall depression levels (Harvard Health Publishing, 2019). Engaging in physical activity additionally leads to the release of endorphins, dopamine, and serotonin, all of which contribute to the regulation of one's mood. These substances are accountable for inducing feelings of pleasure and contentment (Collins, 2017). In essence, engaging in physical activity can lead to long-term feelings of increased happiness.

Mindful Movement

Engaging in walking can be regarded as a viable method for cultivating mindfulness as well. Furthermore, there exists a widespread convention of engaging in the meditative technique known as walking meditation (Greater Good in Action). 2018). Never heard of it? This book was specifically crafted with the intention of fulfilling this purpose. As previously elucidated, the practice of mindfulness should permeate all aspects of one's endeavors. Walking meditation is simply mindful walking, and it's fairly easy to do.

Commence by locating a pathway that permits you to proceed approximately five or six meters in a forward direction. This designated route shall serve as the trajectory for your walking meditation. Your task is to traverse this path, execute a turn, retrace your steps, and continue to repeat this cycle for a duration of ten minutes. The distinction between seated meditation and walking meditation is evidently based on the element of movement involved. Whilst engaged in the practice of meditation in a seated position, one is capable of cultivating a heightened state of awareness with regards to the breath, bodily sensations, and the environment. In the practice of walking meditation, one maintains mindfulness of those very elements and the intricacies involved in traversing the path.

After you have discovered your chosen direction, commence walking with intention and mindfulness. May I inquire about which foot leads the way initially and how would you describe the sensation when the heel makes contact with the ground? Take note of the manner in which your leg gracefully propels forward to initiate the subsequent step, as well as the rhythm and tempo of your movement. It is a compelling encounter when one grasps the fact that they possess the ability to ambulate, yet may have never accorded any deliberate focus to the manner in which they execute locomotion.

This walking regimen provides an effective means of mobilizing the body and cultivating mindfulness. Upon establishing a regular practice of daily physical activity, you will inevitably experience instances where you feel a profound sense of accomplishment in regards to the diligent effort you invest in self-care. Attaining a state of well-being necessitates the maintenance of a sound physique, thereby contributing to a holistic and positive outlook on life.

Physical well-being is additionally associated with a sense of dignity. As an illustration, if you were to have a professional engagement with a prominent corporate organization, it would be inappropriate to present yourself attired in casual sweatpants and a t-shirt with evident signs of wear and perspiration marks. You would present yourself in a hygienic state, attired in a manner that radiates professionalism, and display exemplary traits. An organization will not recruit an individual who neglects personal appearance and hygiene, as it raises doubts about their sense of self-discipline and self-respect. If one cannot muster the effort to wear a tidy shirt, it raises questions about their overall commitment to presenting themselves in a professional manner. This principle applies equally to upholding a consistent exercise regimen. It is unreasonable to anticipate optimal functioning of your mind or physique if you have neglected their care.

To all fitness enthusiasts perusing these words, it is conceivable that this particular segment of the book may elicit a sense of skepticism, as you already possess the inherent drive to engage in physical exercise. Given that you maintain a consistent exercise routine, there may be limited incentive for you to continue reading the remainder of this chapter, wouldn't you agree? Wrong. Merely engaging in regular physical activity does not guarantee that one is engaging in mindful exercise.

Engaging in physical activity is a separate matter from doing so with mindful awareness. Regardless of whether you engage in treadmill running, weightlifting, or attend regular Pilates sessions, you may be unaware of the physiological and mental changes taking place within your body during exercise. Engaging in cautious physical activity necessitates careful attention to both the body and mind during the process. One might assume that it is an inherent expectation to maintain focus while engaging in physical exercise, as it involves numerous distinct motions. You are required to engage in weightlifting or maintain a brisk pace on the treadmill, while also being conscientious of your posture during squat exercises. Nevertheless, this is not the situation.

Whilst engaging in physical activity, there is a higher probability of operating in a state of automaticity. This occurrence transpires when the body and mind acquire such a pronounced level of familiarity with a particular routine that one is able to disengage and enter a state of detachment while performing the task, ultimately allowing the body to seamlessly carry on with the routine in the absence of significant attention. Matters of this nature were deliberated in the preceding chapter pertaining to the subject of meditation. Therefore, assuming one adheres to a reasonably rigorous exercise regimen, it is conceivable that the body may have developed sufficient familiarity with the physical activities, thereby enabling one to become deeply immersed in contemplation. Possibly, this may be something with which you are acquainted. It has been noticed that one's workout on the treadmill has unexpectedly concluded, despite a lack of recollection of extensively engaging in running activities.

This implies that one is engaging in physical activity without conscious awareness. It is not an infrequent occurrence. Frequently, engaging in physical activity can prove to be arduous, thus it becomes more effortless to disengage from our surroundings and divert our focus towards our thoughts, neglecting to attend to the sensations experienced by our bodies. Nevertheless, integrating mindfulness into your exercise regimen empowers you to exert a greater level of mastery over your physical being. Maintaining a conscious awareness of the intricate functioning of your muscles during various physical activities such as running, squatting, or weightlifting enables you to pause and appreciate the rigorous exertion that your body undergoes, as well as the dedicated efforts required to enhance your physical prowess and endurance.

In your subsequent treadmill workout sessions, make a deliberate effort to closely observe and acknowledge the sensations associated with running. In which region of your lower limbs do you experience the greatest sensation? How do you utilize your upper limbs? Direct your gaze towards your lower extremities as they progress on the treadmill, and observe their diligent efforts. Please be attentive and aware of the exertion involved in executing this activity, utilizing your breath as a stabilizing force throughout. This can be equally accomplished when engaging in weightlifting. What transpires within your muscular system upon lifting a weight of substantial magnitude? Can you perceive the flexing and contracting of your muscles? What is the sensation experienced when the weight is returned to its original position and the muscular tension subsides? What is the impact on the remaining parts of your body during weightlifting? Are you engaging your core muscles or contracting your facial muscles? To summarize, what is the genuine sensation of exerting oneself and pushing the limits of one's physical capabilities? In what location do you perceive the sensation and what is its nature?

If you happen to possess contrasting attributes to those of an extremely health-conscious individual and have found the previous few passages to be incomprehensible, rest assured. You are not alone, and there exists a considerable number of individuals who share similar experiences as you. Do not despair, there remains potential for improvement. Simply because you do not gravitate towards exercise and harbor aversion towards walking does not suggest that alternatives are nonexistent. Yoga practice could potentially be an advantageous pursuit for you.

Yoga is a physical discipline that fosters deliberate body movements and contemplative reflection throughout its routines. The genesis of yoga can be traced back to ancient India, dating back more than 5,000 years. In contemporary times, the practice of yoga has gained global popularity and is widely acknowledged for its potential to enhance muscular strength and flexibility. Additionally, it is acknowledged to provide support in matters pertaining to mental well-being, encompassing conditions such as anxiety, stress, and depression (American Osteopathic Association). 2018). During the practice of yoga, individuals are encouraged to exhibit a heightened awareness of their movements, breathing patterns, and their physical experience of poses and stretches. Consequently, yoga cultivates a deeply mindful state, rendering it a highly introspective and contemplative pursuit.

Engaging in yoga helps to maintain motivation as it allows for goal-setting and progress monitoring. Yoga enhances physical strength and flexibility. Upon embarking on your yoga practice, it is imperative to acknowledge that certain postures may prove challenging for your body due to limitations in flexibility or strength. As you progress in your training, you will discern alterations in your physique. Over time and with consistent practice, you will find that tasks previously challenging become increasingly manageable. Initially, it might have been challenging for you to perform a full forward bend and touch your toes. However, once you experience the sensation of your fingertips lightly grazing the tip of your toes, you will perceive the tangible evidence of the strides you have made in your flexibility journey.

Occasionally, it is necessary for us to witness these alterations in order to maintain our motivation. Nevertheless, alterations in the physique and psyche do not occur instantaneously. Attending a single yoga class does not guarantee immediate proficiency in headstand posture. It requires committed application and self-control. You are required to cultivate self-motivation and determination in order to persevere. Do not relinquish your efforts or become disheartened due to the absence of visible or discernible changes within a short span of a few days or weeks.

This similarly applies to your meditation practice. Do not entertain the notion that undergoing a mere week of meditation will result in a complete transformation of your character, accompanied by a profound shift in your perspective of existence. That is not how it functions. The alterations will be minor in nature, rendering them potentially imperceptible upon initial observation. Maintain a clear perspective on the underlying purpose behind your actions—for dedicating ten minutes each day, for engaging in walks, for even embarking on this book's journey.

Reiterate the fact that you are engaging in this endeavor to enhance your quality of life and enhance your emotional well-being.

If you have reached this point in the chapter, it is indicative that you have not been excessively repelled by the notion of incorporating exercise into your lifestyle, which is a positive indicator. Although the amount of information presented may appear overwhelming, it primarily revolves around discarding unhealthy practices and embracing beneficial ones.

It is imperative to bear in mind, throughout the entirety of this process, that cultivating patience within oneself is crucial, while also endeavoring to approach each task without any form of critical judgment. Establishing a habit can be a challenging endeavor, particularly when it pertains to activities that require physical exertion, as they prove to be even more arduous to incorporate into our daily routines. The prevailing justification is a lack of time, fatigue, or a sheer absence of inclination. Nevertheless, it is important to bear in mind that progress is not achieved by offering justifications. As previously stated in the introductory section of this book, it should be acknowledged that reading it will not offer a hastily applied remedy. In order to transform your lifestyle, you will need to exert diligent effort.

Mindfulness Meditation

Meditation ought not to be perceived as an educational process. It should be considered as a process of experiential nature. One should refrain from attempting to acquire knowledge through meditation, and instead, focus on experiencing it. Meditation is an expression of the state of nonduality. The technique you are employing must not be viewed as distinct from your being; it is an inherent part of you, as you are synonymous with the technique itself. The meditator and the act of meditation are inherently intertwined. There is no interconnection."

~Chogyam Trungpa

J

Merely allocating a mere five minutes each day. You can do this. This serves as the cornerstone of your mindfulness practice.

To commence, simply select a suitable moment and assume a seated position. How about right now?

The process is quite straightforward and there is no cause for apprehension, I assure you.

Many individuals find meditation intimidating due to the confrontation with the sheer volume of thoughts that inundate our minds at any given moment. The concept, however, entails acknowledging these thoughts while refraining from excessive attachment, and avoiding the act of forcibly dismissing them. Meditation can be easily practiced by adhering to the instructions outlined below. I highly recommend that you commence without delay. There is no better time than the present.

Prior to commencing, please initiate the use of a timer. I prefer utilizing my smartphone by adjusting its settings and subsequently muting all audible notifications. I intentionally position it beyond access, as a precautionary measure against succumbing to the temptation to ascertain the remaining duration. It is advisable to engage in meditation during a time and in a location where potential distractions can be minimized. However, if circumstances make it inevitable to meditate in the presence of distractions, it is preferable to practice mindfulness in that very moment rather than repeatedly postponing it in pursuit of an ideal environment of complete silence.

Now let's get started...

1. POSTURE. Take a comfortable seat. No additional equipment is required; simply adopt a suitable posture that promotes a straight back, ensuring there is adequate support beneath you, whether it be the floor if you choose to sit there or a chair if you prefer to maintain an upright position. If you so choose, you may adopt

a reclined posture, although there is a possibility that this might transition your meditative experience into a slumber. In the event that you possess a towel or cushion within reach, it may be advantageous to elevate your sitting position slightly (if you are seated on the ground). Maintaining the hips at a higher level relative to the knees promotes a greater degree of comfort and sustainability in your posture. It is crucial to maintain a straight posture of your back. There should be a perception of dual occurrences unfolding concurrently: a vertical expansion towards the heavens and a stable connection to the ground beneath. It is as if there is a force exerting equal tension on either end of your spinal cord. After you have settled comfortably into your seat, inhale deeply and, upon exhaling, allow your shoulder and facial muscles to release and unwind, as they typically remain tense throughout the course of our daily activities.

2. GAZE. You have the option of either maintaining a gentle gaze with your eyes open, or closing them. This is solely a matter of personal preference, therefore it is advised not to dwell excessively on the subject. I prefer to maintain a vigilant state, directing my eyes downwards as I observe my surroundings. This is intended to minimize eye activity, as they remain open while maintaining a state of restfulness. It may be found that maintaining closed eyes facilitates enhanced concentration. Do not hesitate to experiment with both approaches.

3. BREATH. Now, at this juncture, is when the practice of meditation commences. Notice your breath. Do not attempt to decelerate its pace or quantify each occurrence; simply

observe it. Simply focus your attention on the inhalation and exhalation of your breath. Numerous meditation techniques exist, encompassing diverse aspects such as regulating one's breath, utilizing mantras, or engaging in visualizations. However, let us commence by directing our focus towards our breath as it naturally occurs. With each inhalation and exhalation, we remain conscious. Inhaling, exhaling...we observe.

4. THOUGHTS. Undoubtedly, you will begin to observe your thoughts intrude upon the tranquil sanctity of your breathing. A multitude of items will appear. The constant repetition of your daily experiences, a persistent concern that has been troubling you, and even forgotten memories from your childhood that have long been dormant. These thoughts might elicit a slight discomfort, and that is perfectly

acceptable. Throughout the course of our daily lives, it is a common inclination for individuals to seek out distractions as a means to divert their attention from such thoughts. We retrieve our smartphones and proceed to peruse Instagram, we procure a package of Doritos, and commence the act of nibbling on the corner of our lip. However, throughout this designated five-minute interval, we will engage in a meditative practice where we will calmly focus on our breath and allow fleeting thoughts to naturally dissipate. Because guess what? They are just thoughts. They are moving past us in a manner reminiscent of the automobiles we previously discussed on the expressway. They are oscillating in our field of vision akin to the images projected on our television screen. Thus, when you observe any arising thoughts, kindly recognize them, but subsequently redirect your focus gently towards your breathing.

5. BE GENTLE. Make a sincere effort to maintain your attention on your breath and avoid becoming disheartened in the event that your thoughts distract you. Your breath remains a steadfast anchor, ever present for your return. Return to your seat and engage in mindful respiration.

And thus, the fundamental principles of meditation have been presented to you. You have the capacity to allocate five minutes each day; I have confidence in your ability to do so. I urge you to commit yourself to establishing a specific timeframe for this task and faithfully abiding by that commitment to yourself.

Congratulations, you have acquired knowledge on the practice of meditation.

In subsequent instances, you may consider prolonging your sitting duration, acquiring a personalized cushion such as a zafu, or experimenting with alternative approaches. However, armed with this foundational knowledge, you are now equipped to commence immediately.

Feel free to attempt it now prior to proceeding to mindfulness techniques.

The Enhancing Effects Of Meditation On Quality Of Life

In essence, meditation is the condition in which the mind remains untroubled and devoid of disturbances. In times when the level of stress becomes overwhelming, it is imperative for individuals to seek coping mechanisms to alleviate its impact. Certain individuals resort to external stimuli as a means of diverting their minds from concerns, in contrast to others who depend on the practice of meditation to silence their thoughts. Meditation facilitates the process of gaining mastery over one's thoughts, enabling the regulation of emotions.

A multitude of research studies substantiate the remarkable advantages that regular meditation can bestow upon individuals' lives. It serves not only as a mechanism for self-discovery but also as an opportunity to cultivate a sense of empowerment. If you are still uncertain about the suitability of incorporating meditation into your routine, the following enumerates several distinct manners in which it can contribute to enhancing your overall well-being.

Improves focus and concentration

If you consistently experience frequent distractions, even minor ones, it is imperative to regain control of your thoughts. Meditation enhances cognitive attentiveness and concentration, allowing individuals to effectively perform tasks in a timely manner. Frequently, our thoughts become excessively preoccupied with external distractions, causing difficulties in maintaining singular focus. Research indicates that multitasking is no longer effective, therefore, to enhance cognitive capabilities, it is imperative to cultivate concentration and focus on performing tasks individually.

Promotes self-awareness

Regular meditation not only aids in mental clarity. Moreover, it contributes to the development of one's self-awareness. It has the potential to facilitate a deep understanding and awareness of your true essence. Meditation is a powerful tool that not only enhances self-awareness but also aids in the identification and resolution of personal weaknesses, resulting in a clarified state of mind conducive to personal growth and improvement. Engaging in self-exploration is perhaps the most efficacious means of cultivating a sense of ease and acceptance within oneself.

Increases acceptance

Experts assert that cultivating acceptance is an essential skill for enhancing one's well-being, and an avenue towards experiencing greater happiness can be found in the practice of meditation. Engaging in meditation facilitates the embracing of life in its true essence. When delving into one's introspective realm, a profound realization may emerge: certain aspects of one's existence elude the grasp of personal control. You ultimately cease your efforts to resist and acquire the ability to relinquish control and effortlessly adapt to the prevailing circumstances. Though it might require a significant span of one's lifetime, once an individual embarks on the path of self-acceptance, their capacity to embrace others and circumstances tends to enhance significantly.

Encourages a healthier lifestyle

By providing you with the necessary focus and balance, meditation obviates the necessity of relying on external aids to attain the serenity one seeks. Rather than indulging in sugary and fatty foods, you will acquire a preference for wholesome and unprocessed fresh culinary items. Furthermore, it would be advantageous for you to reduce your consumption of alcoholic beverages during periods of stress. In addition, there are individuals who have chosen to abandon the habit of smoking due to their perception of its diminishing significance. When embarking on the practice of meditation, one may aspire to attain a state of improved well-being and enhanced health compared to their initial starting point.

Combats the effects of aging

Research indicates that engagement in meditation exercises can exert a profound influence on neural functioning, to the extent that it can effectively decelerate the aging process. Empirical evidence has shown that individuals who engage in regular meditation exhibit a greater volume of gray matter, colloquially referred to as brain cells. Greater presence of gray matter in an individual corresponds to an enhanced capacity to effectively cope with stress, consequently affording them an improved opportunity to counteract any manifestations of aging.

Although meditation may not serve as a panacea for an improved life, it undeniably possesses immense efficacy as a powerful instrument that can aid individuals in attaining their desired state of being. Do not allow the adversities of life to weigh you down. I advise allocating a few minutes of your daily routine to engage in the practice of meditation, as it will promptly yield numerous advantageous outcomes.

Guided Meditations For Love

I. Introduction to the Meditation for Unlocking the Heart

Please take a moment to settle into a comfortable position. Please take a seat, gently close your eyes, and ensure that your back is neither excessively arched nor strained.

Inhale deeply and endeavor to attain a state of relaxation in various areas of your body. Please remain patient until your energy stabilizes and you begin to attune yourself to the present moment.

Anticipate the emergence of expressions that flow effortlessly from the depths of your soul. Permit your heart to articulate its profound yearnings. Is there anything you have longed for, cherished in your heart throughout the entirety of your existence? Have you harbored any desires that you have consistently hesitated to address? Allow your emotions to articulate desires that you have hesitated to vocalize.

"May I find love"

"May I find happiness"

May I have the privilege of pursuing a life of ease and comfort?"

May experience a sense of fulfillment within the span of their lifetime."

Kindly engage in the deliberate repetition of your selected phrases. Allow your thoughts to find solace within these expressions. Please do not be concerned if your focus begins to drift. Should you reach a juncture where you sense a disconnection, please feel at liberty to release and commence anew.

May I experience love, happiness, and live a life free of hardship.

Make an effort to recollect an individual whom you hold significant affection for. An individual who has consistently provided unwavering support during difficult times. An individual who serves as a source of inspiration and continues to motivate you to fulfill your utmost capabilities. As you engage in the process of visualization, kindly utter the name of the respective individual softly within the confines of your thoughts. Make an effort to sense his presence and send affectionate thoughts towards him.

May you receive affection, experience joy, and navigate through life with grace

Please focus your attention on an individual who has been facing considerable challenges in recent days. An individual who has undergone sorrow, unhappiness, letdown, or resentment. An individual experiencing a challenging circumstance. Envision this individual positioned in front of you. Whisper the name of this individual softly to yourself, while embracing affectionate sentiments towards them.

May you experience the embrace of love, find eternal happiness, and maneuver through life with utmost tranquility

Consider an individual whom you have yet to acquaint yourself with to a considerable extent, but who nevertheless holds significance and influence in your day-to-day existence. An individual whom you would encounter in passing, without fully acknowledging or acknowledging the individual's presence. An individual towards whom you maintain a stance of impartial emotions. This individual may be someone with whom one has infrequent encounters, such as the cashier at a local supermarket or the attendant at a gas station. As you envision his or her presence before you, kindly offer heartfelt sentiments in his or her direction.

May you receive abundant love, experience boundless happiness, and navigate through life with effortless ease.

By utilizing these expressions, we are extending our emotional openness to those around us. We are extending our sphere of benevolence to encompass others, rather than marginalizing them. We are reestablishing a connection with them, instead of disregarding their presence. We are instilling in ourselves the values of compassion and empathy, as opposed to cultivating a sense of apathy. We are extending our compassion to all sentient beings universally, transcending all notions of categorization or division.

May we receive affection, find joy, and experience a sense of tranquility in our lives.

This is intended for all living beings that inhabit this planet - including humans, animals, and all other organisms, regardless of their proximity. Regardless of whether it is known or unknown to us. All forms of life existing on the planet, encompassing those inhabiting land, water, and the atmosphere. Those who are born to those who are passing away. All organisms participating in the cycle of existence.

May we experience love, happiness, and lead a life of utmost tranquility

You are presently experiencing the proliferation of an exceptional energy that radiates from your heart to boundless reaches of the globe. The energy is permeating in all directions, encompassing both the anterior and posterior, as well as the superior and inferior aspects. It appears as though your heart is expanding in limitless ways beyond your previous expectations.

May all individuals be regarded with affection, experience contentment, and navigate through existence with tranquility.

Once you are prepared, cautiously begin to open your eyes and allow the profound vitality to emanate within you for the remainder of the day. Maintain a hopeful mindset, anticipating favorable outcomes that lie ahead.

Heart Healing Meditation

Initiate the practice of meditation by engaging in a gradual and deliberate inhalation and exhalation of breath. Inhale softly, and subsequently exhale.
Direct your attention to your cardiac region. As you engage in a gradual inhalation, endeavor to mentally conceive of your cardiac region expanding and unfurling. Exhale, discarding all pessimistic thoughts into the currents of the wind. Permit the gates of your heart to widen, embracing an influx of boundless love and radiant luminescence beyond the reaches of your imagination. Envision the reassembly of your fractured heart, with its myriad fragments reunited.

Please utilize this period as an opportunity to facilitate the process of emotional restoration within your heart. Release the burdens of previous pains and errors, and permit the radiance permeating your heart to mend your afflictions. This illumination shall serve to augment your strength in the present. This illumination will aid in the restoration of your personal identity, which shall remain inviolable henceforth.

In the event that you experience discomfort in different regions of your physique, envisage this identical illumination journeying to those specific areas. Permit the illumination to permeate and facilitate the healing process in those regions. Envision the complete healing of your heart and body. Envision the affection and illumination radiating outward as it traverses from the depths of your heart to encompass the entirety of each individual cell within your being. In this present moment, let the sensation of tranquility envelop every aspect of your being.

During this exercise, you may experience a sudden surge of emotions, encompassing both positive and negative states. Embrace the opportunity to immerse yourself in this experience and recognize its inherent naturalness. When one experiences a sense of being overwhelmed, adopting the perspective of an impartial observer can prove beneficial, enabling the emotions to unfold naturally. Allow it to rise to the surface and focus on releasing it.

Engage in a series of gentle and deep inhalations and exhalations until the intensity of your emotions has diminished. Envision the infusion of profound affection, radiance, and comprehensive recuperation permeating your entire being. This marks the commencement of a rejuvenated chapter in your existence—the inception of a pristine existence and an evolved individual. Grant yourself the opportunity to embrace and immerse in the radiance of forthcoming prospects.

Presented here are several affirmations that you may find beneficial as you embrace your newfound existence.

"I am healing now. Body, mind, and spirit"

I have relinquished my attachments to previous events. I have relinquished all the pain and errors from my life at present.

I am recovering my well-being. I am currently in the process of recognizing the significance of prioritizing my physical and mental well-being, as it serves as the fundamental framework for all aspects of my life.

The present moment offers a propitious opportunity to relinquish the past and embrace the current circumstances. The desired future that I have long aspired to is within my grasp"

The potency of luminosity and affection is bestowing upon me a curative influence. I express my gratitude for the chance to experience healing in this circumstance."

Upon concluding this meditative practice, imagine the illumination enveloping your heart, reinstating it to its natural condition.

Once you feel prepared, softly open your eyes and reintegrate yourself into a state of consciousness.

Number five - Recognizing the forebears

Virtually every culture worldwide places significant emphasis on showing reverence and recognition towards their forebears. Upon reflecting on history, it becomes evident that ancient civilizations, such as those in the Stone Age around 2.5 million years ago, held a deep reverence for both the natural elements and the departed. Throughout the emergence of diverse civilizations and faith systems, the veneration and deference towards our forebears have consistently permeated our existence. It is imperative to acknowledge our ancestors, as our existence and inherent qualities stem from their affection and innate inclination to reproduce. Most of the characteristics and attributes we have inherited from our ancestors undoubtedly contribute to the ease and seamlessness with which we navigate through life. Furthermore, their continual endeavors and hardships play a significant role in our ongoing development, much like their unwavering support propels us forward in the form of positive energy. They committed numerous errors, gained valuable insights from them, and imprinted this wisdom within their genetic code. These indelible manifestations of knowledge are undeniably contributing to our endeavors, albeit perhaps not yet within the purview of our consciousness.

No progenitor would ever wish to witness the enduring agony of their forthcoming progeny. The manifestation of suffering occurs solely when an individual in the subsequent generation has inherited those imprints of distress from ancestral DNA, leading to their personal experience of adversity. However, even in such cases, when we express love, gratitude, respect, and honor towards our ancestors' energy, they unfailingly return to us, bestowing blessings upon us and aiding us in overcoming our challenges. There have been myriad instances wherein we perceive the presence of our grandparents or any other predecessor within our dream state, endeavoring to establish a form of communication with us. On certain occasions in the realm of dreams, manifestations emerge that impart resolutions to the predicaments we encounter and experience a sense of confinement. Indeed, on numerous occasions we can perceive their presence and magnified vitality during moments of adversity. They exist within us and remain constantly prepared to provide assistance. However, it is important to note that one should not display a self-centered attitude by solely relying on their assistance in times of crisis. In lieu of this, what they truly require is an untainted heart characterized by genuine love and profound respect. Their role within our lives should be etched enduringly within the depths of our hearts.

Undoubtedly, there exist multiple avenues through which appreciation can be demonstrated towards them. Across diverse regions of the globe, numerous ceremonial practices are established to commemorate the venerable spirits. As an illustration, India encompasses a multitude of customs and ceremonial practices, such as the revered tradition of PitruTarpan and a plethora of others. However, it is crucial to bear in mind these individuals within ourselves, as our forebears continue to exist within us. The DNA containing their imprints resides within us, thus their presence persists in an energetic form within us. Therefore, it is imperative to recognize and appreciate this inherent vitality, and what better method exists than engaging in meditative practices while attuned to their energies.

When individuals engage in a meditative practice in conjunction with the energies emanating from their forebears, they experience a profound state of unity with every constituent element comprising their ancestors' being. It essentially entails a profound connection with the Family System, wherein one is able to tap into an extensive wellspring of wisdom in addition to receiving boundless affection.

The subsequent contemplation aims to establish a reconnection with our predecessors, encompassing those who are part of our familial lineage and DNA composition. It is a deeply heartfelt gesture of our spirit to express our appreciation, esteem, and reverence. If this motion is executed amidst the natural surroundings, encompassing all the elemental forces and accompanied by other familial individuals, the effect is a deep and illuminating experience.

Meditation:

1) Assume a seated position in which your legs are extended, making contact with the floor, and your spinal column is impeccably aligned.
2) Gently shut your eyes and inhale deeply a few times. Inhale through your nasal passage and exhale through your oral cavity. Release any extraneous thoughts occupying your mind and simply allow yourself to unwind.
3) Achieve a state of inner alignment and experience a profound sense of grounding to the Earth Element, while simultaneously establishing a profound connection to the omnipresent universal energies of the Cosmos. Experience the vital force of the Earth element and the cosmic fabric permeating your being.

Allow every inhalation to channel this vitality throughout every single cell, tissue, muscle, bone, and organ within your body.

4) In the event that any unwelcome thoughts persist, simply relinquish them.

5) In the current state of relaxation, position your index and middle fingers

Place your right hand to the right of the navel. Inhale deeply.

6) In the depths of your heart, express gratitude to your forebears

All that has been bestowed upon me by you. I wholeheartedly embrace all bestowed upon me with deep appreciation, reverence, and dignity."

7) Inhale deeply once more, allowing yourself to experience the sensation of receiving everything.

Endowed with the inheritance bestowed upon you by your forebears, yet imbued with sentiments of affection and empathy. Cultivate a more inclusive and receptive stance towards it.

8) Maintaining the current finger placement, proceed in silence

Your heart expresses a profound commitment to welcoming all (i.e. ancestors) into the depths of its love, reverence, appreciation, and esteem.

9) Inhale deeply once more and mentally express profound reverence to all individuals

The forebears have bestowed upon them this esteemed position characterized by love, gratitude, respect, and honor. Experience all of these emotions as you humbly submit to their influence.

10) While maintaining the position of your fingers unchanged, silently

My heart proclaims, "I hereby reclaim my position within the family structure." If I have assumed the role of my parents, grandparents, or ancestors, I release it at this moment and reclaim my own position."

11) Psychologically, be receptive to this energetic transformation. While you may not be cognizant of it in your conscious state, it is a certainty that any necessary alterations will inevitably transpire.

12) Once more, inhale deeply and, within the depths of your heart, affirm in complete silence, "If I have assumed any afflictions borne by any individual within my familial lineage, I hereby elect to release them in this present moment."

13) Exhale any afflictions that may have entered your realm via your genetic code. Grant yourself the opportunity to relinquish it entirely.

14) Once more, lower your head slighty and inwardly express gratitude to my forebears for their assistance. I express my heartfelt gratitude to you for bestowing upon me this cherished

existence. I am determined to make the most of the opportunity presented to me in this lifetime by engaging in meaningful endeavors."

15) Now, kindly place both of your hands gently upon your thighs and assume a comfortable seated posture. Enable the assimilation of the recently discovered energies within oneself. Upon achieving internal integration, you may proceed to open your eyes.

This meditation serves as a fundamental practice to establish a connection with our ancestral energies, while also demonstrating the proper reverence they rightfully deserve. When individuals engage in meditation and direct their focus towards their ancestors, they will experience a profound surge of energy within themselves; however, this energy is characterized by a tranquil nature. This meditative practice can provide assistance in relinquishing ambiguous distractions when expressing gratitude towards an individual whose identity remains uncertain. Furthermore, as you relinquish the burdens that you have shouldered, a significant portion of the disruptive energy inherently dissolves. I recommend engaging in this meditation practice for a minimum of 21 consecutive days to facilitate the process of rewiring your mind and establishing fresh foundations of affirmative energy.

Acknowledging our Territorial Ancestors:
Similar to how our genealogical lineage consists of ancestors such as grandparents, great grandparents, and great great grandparents, we also possess "Territorial Ancestors". These individuals are past residents of a specific geographical region. They may

also be referred to as the ethereal entities or custodial figures of the terrain, in addition to being recognized as ancestral predecessors of the region. They represent the progenitors who previously inhabited the land and experienced a range of affectionate encounters and distressing events. In numerous cultures, a prevalent belief is held that these ancestral spirits are believed to be existent within the very atmosphere we respire. They are consistently engaging in communication with us, whether or not we are cognizant of it. A demonstration of connecting with our ancestral roots can be observed through the presence of a venerable mango tree. This mango tree not only symbolizes an antiquated emblem, but also holds the inherent spirit of the ancestral heritage associated with this territory. It encompasses the lasting impressions of all the diverse experiences that these individuals have undergone, be it instances of trauma, conflict, joy, profound unity, or festive occasions. Regardless of what it may have been, everything pertaining to it is present.

Due to the increased mobility in our contemporary society, only a limited number of individuals have the opportunity to grow up in close proximity to the ancestral lands of their predecessors. A significant number of individuals relocate to different towns and cities in search of improved opportunities or to establish their families in environments offering superior amenities and a more elevated quality of life. However, it is important to note that our predecessors resided on those territories, which we refer to as our ancestral abode. The caretakers of that territory diligently attended to our forebears, bestowing upon them not only their presence, but also the intangible inheritance of emotions, sentiments, imprints, and life experiences. And now we possess it internally. It is of paramount importance to recognize and pay homage to the indigenous predecessors of the territory, in conjunction with the current inhabitants. As an illustration, it can be noted that your birthplace is India, whereas your forebears hailed from what is now known as Pakistan. Subsequently, it is incumbent upon you to recognize both India and Pakistan. Although you yourself did not directly experience life in Pakistan, your ancestors were indeed connected to that country. Recognizing and honoring the territories will foster harmony and affection within the society.

In the below-mentioned exercise, it comprises two distinct components. The initial concept entails recognizing and honoring the geographical area where your predecessors resided, whereas the latter refers to the geographic region in which you currently dwell. This practice of movement or meditation can be undertaken in solitude or in the company of one's entire family, enabling each participant to establish a profound connection with the land and express their heartfelt reverence towards the ancestral inhabitants of the territory.

Once you have become comfortably situated, subtly retract your chin. It is advised against directing one's gaze upward as it can potentially result in strain on the neck muscles. In addition, it is important to avoid directing your gaze entirely downwards towards the ground or your lap, as this can similarly strain your neck and cause rapid fatigue. Keeping the chin gently tucked is indicative of a humble disposition, contributing to one's state of groundedness, thus aligning with the fundamental aims of the practice of meditation.

Maintain the position of your tongue against the palate within your oral cavity to facilitate unobstructed respiration, followed by the gradual release of tension in your facial musculature to slightly unlock your jaw. It is important to avoid excessive looseness or tightness in its hanging configuration. This action promotes facial relaxation and improved respiration, ultimately enhancing concentration during the activity.

Furthermore, it is necessary to softly ease the tension in your vision, directing it approximately 2 to 4 feet ahead, specifically focused on the floor, maintaining a state of calmness. Please refrain from fixating on any specific object or excessively concentrating on the wall art or carpet on the floor. Instead, adopt a more relaxed approach by maintaining a loosely directed gaze and easing the strain on your eyes. If you so desire, you may also choose to occlude your vision, thereby mitigating potential distractions emanating from the ambient luminosity or any other elements within the environs.

Prior to commencing your meditation practice, it is advisable to consciously determine whether you wish to close your eyes or maintain them in an open position. This will help prevent any potential restless impulses to either open or close your eyes during the meditation session. Engaging in fidgeting serves as a hindrance to your focused practice and undermines your ability to concentrate. Therefore, it is recommended that you either maintain an open-eyed or closed-eyed state, and once a choice has been made, steadfastly adhere to it. Nevertheless, should you find it excessively challenging to maintain visual attentiveness throughout the course of the exercise, feel free to close your eyes if you so desire, refraining from placing excessive strain upon yourself.

Subsequently, it is imperative that you commence engaging in meditative practices. There exist various meditative techniques from which you can choose, however, as a novice, it would be advisable to adhere to simpler and more accessible methods. The subsequent section elucidates a selection of uncomplicated contemplative exercises that can be implemented effortlessly, irrespective of the time of day or location.

www.ingramcontent.com/pod-product-compliance
Lightning Source LLC
Chambersburg PA
CBHW050238120526
44590CB00016B/2133